From Religion to Relationship

Healing Your Faith Journey

Rhaegine Valero

From Religion to Relationship: Healing Your Faith Journey

Copyright © 2025 Rhaegine Valero

All rights reserved. No part of this publication may be reproduced, distributed, or transmitted in any form or by any means, including photocopying, recording, or other electronic or mechanical methods, without the prior written permission of the author, except in the case of brief quotations embodied in critical reviews and certain other non-commercial uses permitted by copyright law.

Table Of Contents

Introduction: *Rediscovering Your Identity in Christ* v

Chapter 1: *Scripture Foundation* 1

Chapter 2: *Creating a Deep, Personal Relationship with Jesus* 5

Chapter 3: *Thy Church and Thy Self* 11

Chapter 4: *Church Manipulation and the Power of Religious Practices* 15

Chapter 5: *The Illusion of Righteousness* 27

Chapter 6: *The Danger of Judging Others Walk with Christ* 35

Chapter 7: *Embracing the Freedom to Question* 47

Chapter 8: *Balancing Church Practices and Personal Identity* 57

Chapter 9: *A Church Home Is Essential for Spiritual Growth* 63

Chapter 10: *Social Media's Influence on Your Authentic Relationship with Christ* 69

Chapter 11: *Trusting God in the Midst of the Struggle* 85

Chapter 12: *Moving Forward with Grace, Truth, and Freedom* 91

Appendices: *Additional Resources for Growth* 97

Introduction:
Rediscovering Your Identity in Christ

I grew up hearing about God, and attending church on and off, but I never truly had a relationship with Him. I didn't understand what it meant to KNOW Him. I was always certain that God existed, yet I spent years searching for Him through different religions and belief systems. I walked away from the Christianity in which I was raised, only to find myself right back in it.

But this time, it was different.

In 2020, I came to know God during a suicide attempt. I baptized myself in the very water I intended to drown in—and to my surprise, as He pulled me out, I received the gift of tongues. Of course, it would be the King of Kings to give me a language to speak directly to Him. Later, on June 18, 2022, I was baptized at The Light House Ministries in Houston, Texas, by Pastor Hammond. This time, it wasn't just an outward declaration—it was a transformation.

The person I once was sank into that water, and the one who rose was who God had destined me to become. As I began my journey, I was filled with passion. I shared the gospel wherever I could. However, I was also desperately trying to transition from sinner to saint overnight. After two years of being on fire for God through trials, tribulations, and relentless striving, I attended Military Chaplain training in California. It was there that I finally realized I was experiencing compassion fatigue. For the first time, I saw the truth: I had clung to a colonized religion to numb the pain of my childhood, trading one wound for another until I lost myself completely.

And then, everything unraveled.

I stopped attending church, abandoned my spiritual videos, and barely prayed. I cursed heavily and even wanted to quit my journey to becoming a Military Chaplain. What I once saw as a phase of disobedience was actually a wake-up call. My faith had been built on a façade. I didn't know who I was in Christ. I idolized the tools, the platform, the pastor, even my calling, mistaking borrowed beliefs for my own. I never questioned what was preached, as if false prophets couldn't exist. I lost myself. My insecurities became loud, and my confidence shattered. I believe in the church, but I also know the dangers of losing yourself in religion. In His mercy, God allowed me to fall into a space of reckoning, a season of silence, and self confrontation.

I felt lost, confused, and guilty. How can I feel this way when God has already done so much for me? It was an uncomfortable awakening, like the world paused while I was being reshaped. I sensed God leading me to an answer, but no matter how desperately I sought Him, He would not respond to me verbally. Yet, His silence led me into the wilderness. It wasn't homelessness or loneliness. It wasn't even the heartbreak from my mother or the weight of my childhood trauma. No, this breaking point came from something I never expected. I had mastered emotional suppression and called it self-control, believing I was walking in righteousness. In corporate America, I endured bullying in silence. In the military, I remained quiet in the face of sexual assault and coercion, never standing up for myself. I mistook passivity for virtue, believing that enduring mistreatment was a mark of spiritual strength. Then one day, God brought me back to the very job where I once suffered in silence. And I finally reached my breaking point. For the first time since being saved, I cried out:

"God, are You really there?"

In that moment, everything changed. God allowed me to break so I could be rebuilt. But first, I had to face my own darkness and be honest about all of me not just the good, obedient parts. In that season, I had nothing. No tools. No church. No distractions.

Only Jesus.

I let myself feel. Instead of suppressing my emotions, I gave myself permission to experience them, especially my anger. I learned to speak up, take up space, and embrace who I truly was. I became still yet radiant. No longer pretending, I released the religion I once clung to and chose to know Jesus for myself. I questioned everything I had been taught, digging deeper into Scripture, and searching for a church that aligned with who I was becoming not who I used to be. After attending various church services and running away from my original church home, I realized something deeper: I had judged my pastor and my church family and ran, carrying unresolved wounds with me. At the end of that season, God brought me right back to the place I always needed.

The Light House Church in Houston, Texas, under the leadership of Pastor Keion Henderson. But this time, I was different. I walked through those church doors no longer trying to fit into anyone else's expectations. I allowed myself to feel. I learned to set boundaries. I refused to normalize abuse. Most importantly, I stopped striving to earn God's love. Now, I want you, the reader, to experience the same freedom. I want you to open the box where you've locked away your true self, the one you silenced just to conform to the world, to religion, to expectations that were never yours to carry.

I want you to accept every part of yourself the good, the bad, the darkness, and the light. Give yourself grace in the sanctification process and understand you do not have to earn God's love. You do not have to idolize a pastor just because you are under their leadership. You are uniquely created in Christ. His love is not something you work for it is a gift you have always possessed.

A gift only He can give.

The purpose of this workbook is to help individuals who have been lost in church roles and religious rituals rediscover their authentic identity in Christ.

Chapter 1:
Scripture Foundation

 **Explore Foundational Scriptures that Declare Our Identity in Christ**

2 Corinthians 5:17 (ESV)

"Therefore, if anyone is in Christ, he is a new creation. The old has passed away; behold, the new has come."

Galatians 2:20 (ESV)

"I have been crucified with Christ. It is no longer I who live, but Christ who lives in me. And the life I now live in the flesh I live by faith in the Son of God, who loved me and gave himself for me."

Romans 8:16 (ESV)

"The Spirit himself bears witness with our spirit that we are children of God."

Your identity is not defined by your roles, performance, or external validation, but by Christ's work in you. Knowing who you are in Christ empowers you to live with confidence, rooted in grace rather than striving.

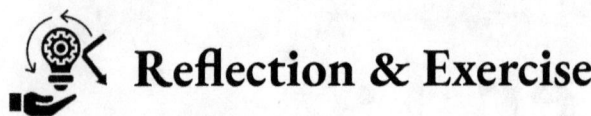 **Reflection & Exercise**

In what areas of your life are you tempted to define yourself by roles or achievements?

_____
_____
_____
_____
_____
_____
_____

What does it mean to you personally to be a "new creation" in Christ?

_____
_____
_____
_____
_____
_____
_____

 **Heart Check**

Are you living as if you are fully accepted by God, or are you still trying to earn His approval through performance?

 **Journal Prompt**

Write a letter to your old self—the version of you that lived under shame, fear, or striving, before truly knowing who you are in Christ. Pour out the lies you believed about your worth, your purpose, and your identity.

Chapter 2:
Creating a Deep, Personal Relationship with Jesus

Building Intimacy: Cultivating a Transformative Connection with Christ

 **Jesus as Your Friend**

Jesus didn't come to establish a set of rituals; He came to restore a relationship. Faith is not just about church attendance or religious knowledge; it's about a living, intimate connection with Jesus Christ. He longs to be your friend, your confidant, your Savior, and your daily companion.

Throughout Scripture, we see moments of deep personal relationship with Jesus. Mary sitting at His feet, the disciples walking and talking with Him, and even His private conversations in prayer. These weren't just religious acts; they were expressions of love, intimacy, and devotion.

Your relationship with Jesus is meant to be deeply personal. It's built in the quiet moments of prayer, the vulnerable cries of your heart, and the daily walk of trust and surrender.

 Scripture

John 15:15 (NIV)

"I no longer call you servants, because a servant does not know his master's business. Instead, I have called you friends, for everything that I learned from my Father I have made known to you."

 **Reflection & Exercise**

How might your life change if you began to see Jesus as your closest friend, someone you confide in, laugh with, and walk beside each day?

If Jesus truly sat beside you as your best friend, what unspoken hurt, fear, or secret would you finally share with him?

 **Heart Check**

Do you approach your relationship with Jesus as a duty—or a delight?

What would it look like to reorder your days, so His presence feels more real than your schedule?

 # Journal Prompt

Write a letter to Jesus and tell Him everything you've been afraid to say out loud. Pour out the anger, the shame, the loneliness, the control you keep clinging to. Admit where you've stopped trusting Him, where you've gone numb, where faith has felt hard.

Chapter 3:
Thy Church and Thy Self

How Institutional Christianity Can Shape Our Identity

 Institutional Pressures

Many churches whether intentionally or unintentionally—place expectations on members that begin to shape identity more than Christ does. These expectations may look like pressure to always serve, conform, attend every event, speak or dress a certain way, or suppress doubts and emotions in the name of "faith." Over time, these cultural norms can create an environment where people feel more like roles than individuals performing for approval rather than growing in grace. True identity isn't found in becoming the "ideal" church member. It's found in being fully known and loved by Jesus.

 **Scripture**

Colossians 2:20-23 (NIV)

"Since you died with Christ to the elemental spiritual forces of this world, why, as though you still belonged to the world, do you submit to its rules: 'Do not handle! Do not taste! Do not touch!'? These rules, which have to do with things that are all destined to perish with use, are based on merely human commands and teachings. Such regulations indeed have an appearance of wisdom, with their self-imposed worship, their false humility, and their harsh treatment of the body, but they lack any value in restraining sensual indulgence."

 **Reflection & Exercise**

In what ways has the church's image of "Holy" made you hide your humanity, questions, grief, or imperfections, from God?

_____

_____

_____

_____

_____

_____

Where have you confused the approval of people with the acceptance of Christ, and how has that shaped your sense of self-worth?

_____

_____

_____

_____

_____

_____

 **Heart Check**

What masks have you worn to stay loved by the church that have kept you from receiving the love God already freely gives?

Chapter 4:
Church Manipulation and the Power of Religious Practices

The Hidden Forces Behind Faith:
How Rituals and Authority Shape Our Actions and Beliefs

 **Understanding Church Manipulation**

Not every church experience reflects Christ's heart. Sometimes, what's meant to be a place of healing becomes a source of harm. Church manipulation happens when leaders or systems use spiritual language, authority, or guilt to control, shame, or pressure people— often under the guise of "obedience," "submission," or "serving God." Instead of guiding people toward Jesus, manipulation distorts the Gospel, making individuals feel like their worth is tied to performance, compliance, or blind loyalty. This kind of spiritual control can leave deep wounds— causing confusion, burnout, fear of questioning leadership, and even fear of God Himself.

 **Scripture**

Matthew 23:4 (NLT)

"They crush people with unbearable religious demands and never lift a finger to ease the burden."

 **Reflection & Exercise**

Have you ever felt pressure to serve, give, or obey in ways that felt rooted in fear rather than love?

How has church-based manipulation affected your view of God and your personal relationship with Him?

 **Heart Check**

How has spiritual manipulation, abuse of authority, or hypocrisy within the church distorted your view of God's character and your trust in Him?

📓 Journal Prompt

Describe a time when someone in spiritual authority used guilt, fear, or control to influence your actions. How did it shape your faith?

 Unmasking False Authority

Jesus never used fear to lead, He led with truth, grace, and love. His harshest rebukes were for religious leaders who misused their authority to burden others while failing to lift a finger to help. False authority operates through fear and control, but the authority of Christ brings freedom and transformation.

 Scripture

Matthew 20:25-28 (ESV)

"But Jesus called them to him and said, 'You know that the rulers of the Gentiles lord it over them, and their great one's exercise authority over them. It shall not be so among you. But whoever would be great among you must be your servant, and whoever would be first among you must be your slave, even as the Son of Man came not to be served but to serve, and to give his life as a ransom for many."

True authority in the Kingdom reflects the heart of a servant. It seeks to empower, not to oppress.

 **Reflection & Exercise**

How can you begin rebuilding trust in spiritual community after experiencing control or spiritual harm?

📝 Journal Prompt

Write a prayer asking God to reveal any false authority you've submitted to intentionally or unintentionally. Invite Him to restore your discernment and help you walk in the freedom and safety of His leadership.

 Shift from Ritual to Relationship

Even good things—like prayer, fasting, or church attendance—can become idols when they are disconnected from intimacy with Christ. When our faith becomes more about outward routines than inward connection, it loses its power to transform. Instead of drawing us closer to Jesus, religious practices can become checklists that feed pride or pressure.

 Scripture

Matthew 23:27-28 (ESV)

"Woe to you, scribes and Pharisees, hypocrites! For you are like whitewashed tombs, which outwardly appear beautiful, but within are full of dead people's bones and all uncleanness. So you also outwardly appear righteous to others, but within you are full of hypocrisy and lawlessness."

Jesus calls us beyond surface-level religion and into a deep, authentic relationship with Him. He isn't looking for perfection—He's longing for presence.

 **Reflection & Exercise**

In what ways have religious routines taken the place of authentic relationships in your spiritual life?

_____
_____
_____
_____
_____
_____
_____

What would it look like to return to the simplicity of walking with Jesus?

_____
_____
_____
_____
_____
_____
_____

 # Journal Prompt

Strip away the polished answers and be raw before God: Are your spiritual rhythms truly a response to His love, or have they become a shield to hide your dryness and distraction?

Chapter 5:
The Illusion of Righteousness

Fighting the "Works" Mentality

 The Temptation to Perform

Many churches inadvertently cultivate a performance-based mindset. This can lead us to believe that we must earn God's love or approval through our works, rituals, or perfect behavior. When we fall into this mentality, we start measuring our worth by our actions rather than resting in the truth that God's love is unconditional. It's important to recognize that the gospel is not about perfection but about grace and transformation.

 Scripture

Ephesians 2:8–9 (ESV)

"For by grace you have been saved through faith. And this is not your own doing; it is the gift of God, not a result of works, so that no one may boast."

 **Reflection & Exercise**

When you think about your relationship with God, do you ever feel pressure to *prove* your love or worth through what you do? What would it look like to simply rest in being loved, without doing anything to deserve it?

 # Biblical Truth: Salvation by Grace Alone

Salvation is not earned through our works but is a gift from God. Ephesians 2:8–9 emphasizes that we are saved by grace through faith, and this is not from ourselves—it is God's gift. Understanding that salvation is a gift rather than a reward for good behavior transforms how we live our Christian life. We no longer strive to earn God's love; instead, we live in gratitude for the love He has already given us.

 # Scripture

Romans 4:4-5 (NIV)

"Now to the one who works, wages are not credited as a gift but as an obligation. However, to the one who does not work but trusts God who justifies the ungodly, their faith is credited as righteousness."

Righteousness is credited through faith, not effort.

 **Reflection & Exercise**

Do you believe that salvation is a gift or do you subconsciously feel like you must "earn" it through works?

 **Heart Check**

In what ways does truly receiving God's grace challenge your self-reliance, reshape your view of others, and transform the way you respond to failure or weakness?

 **Journal Prompt**

Grace is not just a doctrine but an invitation into intimacy with God. Reflect on how truly believing that 'while we were still sinners, Christ died for us' (Romans 5:8) shifts your view of yourself and your faith journey. In what hidden areas do you still strive for approval, mask your weakness, or fear God's disappointment? Write a raw, honest prayer, asking the Lord to rewrite those narratives with His love and to teach you to rest in His finished work at the cross.

Journal Prompt Continued...

Chapter 6:
The Danger of Judging Others Walk with Christ

Understanding the Call to Love, Not Judge

 **Judging Others' Relationship with Christ**

It is easy to judge others' walk with Christ based on our own understanding or personal expectations. Whether it's their level of faith, the way they express their spirituality, or their actions, we often fall into the trap of comparing them to ourselves. This judgment not only reflects a misunderstanding of grace but also creates division within the body of Christ. We must remember that each person's relationship with Jesus is unique and personal. Only God knows the full story of someone's heart, and it is not our place to judge.

 **Scripture**

Romans 2:1 (NIV)

"You, therefore, have no excuse, you who pass judgement on someone else, for at whatever point you judge another, you are condemning yourself, because you who pass judgement do the same things."

 Reflection & Exercise

Reflect on a time when you judged someone else's walk with Christ. What led you to do so, and what was the impact?

_____
_____
_____
_____
_____
_____

How can you focus on extending grace to others rather than judgment, and what steps can you take to build deeper love and understanding?

_____
_____
_____
_____
_____
_____

 # Heart Check

Do you ever measure others by a standard you yourself struggle to meet, rather than by God's grace?

Journal Prompt

Reflect on moments when judgement toward another believer revealed something deeper in your own heart—fear, insecurity, hidden jealousy, or a desire for control. Instead of just recalling what you thought about them, ask: What does this judgement say about what I truly believe about God's grace? Write a confession of those hidden attitudes, then invite God to dismantle them and rebuild your heart to see others through His mercy, not your measure.

Journal Prompt Continued...

 # Self-Righteousness and Scripture

It's easy to use Scripture to justify our own judgments of others. However, when we do this, we risk becoming self-righteous instead of compassionate. Jesus calls us to love one another, and He teaches that our understanding of His Word should lead to humility, not arrogance. When we allow Scripture to become a tool for self-righteous judgment, we miss its true intent, which is to transform our hearts and lead us to love others as Christ loves us.

 # Scripture

Luke 18:9-14 (ESV)

"He also told this parable to some who trusted in themselves that they were righteous and treated others with contempt: 'Two men went up into the temple to pray, one a Pharisee and the other a tax collector. The Pharisee, standing by himself, prayed thus: "God, I thank you that I am not like other men, extortioners, unjust, adulterers, or even like this tax collector. I fast twice a week; I give tithes of all that I get." But the tax collector, standing far off, would not even lift up his eyes to heaven, but beat his breast, saying, "God, be merciful to me, a sinner!" I tell you; this man went down to his house justified, rather than the other. For everyone who exalts himself will be humbled, but the one who humbles himself will be exalted."

Reflection & Exercise

When have you used Scripture as a weapon to feel right instead of as a mirror to be made right? What fear or insecurity were you trying to protect?

_____
_____
_____
_____
_____
_____

How can you use Scripture to grow in humility and love for others rather than to point out their shortcomings?

_____
_____
_____
_____
_____
_____

 **Heart Check**

Have you ever used Scripture to feel superior, prove a point, or mask your own sin?

_____
_____
_____
_____
_____
_____
_____

How can you humble yourself and embrace Scripture as a tool for love and transformation rather than self- righteousness?

_____
_____
_____
_____
_____
_____
_____

Journal Prompt

Recall a time when you used your knowledge of Scripture to protect yourself from conviction instead of allowing it to transform you. What fear or insecurity might have been at the root of that reaction? How might God have been inviting you to see His Word not as a shield for your pride, but as a tool for healing and humility?

 # Scriptural Warning on Judging Others

Jesus' words in Matthew 7:1-5 serve as a clear warning against judging others. He emphasizes that we must first examine our own hearts before pointing out flaws in others. It's not our role to condemn but to love and extend grace, as Christ has done for us. The standard we use to judge others will be used against us, and we must hold ourselves to the same level of grace and mercy we extend to others.

 # Scripture

Matthew 7:1–5 (ESV)

"Judge not, that you be not judged. For with the judgment, you pronounce you will be judged, and with the measure you use it will be measured to you. Why do you see the speck that is in your brother's eye, but do not notice the log that is in your own eye? Or how can you say to your brother, 'Let me take the speck out of your eye,' when there is the log in your own eye? You hypocrite, first take the log out of your own eye, and then you will see clearly to take the speck out of your brother's eye."

 **Journal Prompt**

Think of someone you've written off or labeled unworthy— without ever carrying their burdens or weeping over their wounds. What does that reveal about the state of your own heart and your understanding of God's mercy toward you?

Chapter 7:
Embracing the Freedom to Question

The Fallacy of One "Correct" Interpretation Breaking Free from Dogma: The Empowerment of Diverse Perspectives in Faith

 ## The Truth About Interpretation

For generations, theological discussions have often been framed around the idea that one interpretation is "correct" while all others are "wrong". While God's truth is unchanging, our understanding of it must be approached with humility and openness. Rigid thinking can stifle growth, alienate fellow believers, and reduce rich Scripture into narrow, divisive doctrines.

The truth is, we all come to the Bible with different life experiences, cultural lenses, and levels of maturity in our faith. What if the goal is not to prove we're right, but to discover more of God's heart together? Learning to hold our convictions with grace allows space for authentic dialogue, deeper discovery, and mutual transformation.

 Scripture

1 Corinthians 13:12 (NIV)

"For now we see only a reflection as in a mirror; then we shall see face to face. Now I know in part; then I shall know fully, even as I am fully known."

This verse reminds us that our current understanding is limited. One day we will see clearly—but until then, we are all learning and growing. Grace in interpretation is not compromised; it's Christlike humility.

 **Reflection & Exercise**

Has there ever been a time when your view of Scripture changed through conversation or study? How did it affect your faith journey?

_____

_____

_____

_____

_____

_____

How can you begin to view theological disagreement not as a threat, but as an opportunity for mutual growth?

_____

_____

_____

_____

_____

_____

 **Heart Check**

Am I more focused on being right, or on becoming more like Christ in how I listen, learn, and love others?

 **Journal Prompt**

Reflect on a time when you felt challenged by a different interpretation of Scripture. What did you learn about God, yourself, and the community of faith through that experience? How might it shape the way you approach future conversations?

 # Humility in Theological Conversations

Humility is essential when engaging with Scripture. We're not called to have all the answers—we're called to seek God with open hearts. Even the apostle Paul commended the Bereans for examining his teachings rather than accepting them blindly.

This example reminds us that asking questions, testing interpretations, and diving deeper into Scripture isn't rebellion—it's faith in action. It honors God when we pursue truth with both passion and humility.

 # Scripture

Acts 17:11 (ESV)

"Now these Jews were more noble than those in Thessalonica; they received the word with all eagerness, examining the Scriptures daily to see if these things were so."

Reflection & Exercise

Have you ever held tightly to a particular interpretation without leaving room for other perspectives? How might that have impacted your conversations or growth?

In what ways can you start creating space for healthy, Spirit-led questioning and deeper engagement with Scripture?

 **Heart Check**

Are you more concerned with winning arguments than letting God win your heart? Where might your desire to be right be blinding you to the Spirit's call to repent, listen, and be changed?

Do you invite God into your questions—or do you fear them?

 # Journal Prompt

Write a letter to God expressing any past fears, frustrations, or hesitations you've had about questioning your faith or long-held beliefs. Ask Him to guide you into a deeper relationship with His Word—one rooted in truth, love, and humility. Let this be a moment of spiritual freedom and renewal.

Chapter 8:
Balancing Church Practices and Personal Identity

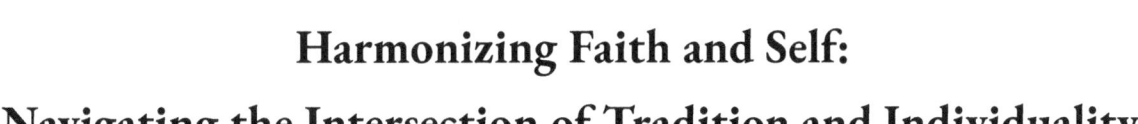

**Harmonizing Faith and Self:
Navigating the Intersection of Tradition and Individuality**

Prayer, fasting, service, and Bible study are powerful spiritual tools meant to help us grow in our relationship with Christ but they were never meant to define our worth or determine our value to God. When we begin to treat these practices as requirements for approval rather than invitations to connection, they can slowly become idols.

We start measuring our holiness by how much we do instead of who we are in Christ. These tools are sacred, but they are not the source of our righteousness—Jesus is. When rightly aligned, they lead us into deeper intimacy with God. When misused, they can trap us in cycles of guilt, performance, and spiritual burnout. The key is remembering that these practices are expressions of relationship, not conditions for love.

 **Scripture**

Romans 5:1 (NIV)

"Therefore, since we have been justified through faith, we have peace with God through our Lord Jesus Christ."

 **Reflection & Exercise**

In what ways have you relied on spiritual practices to feel "worthy" before God?

How can you begin to use these tools as a means of connection rather than a measure of your value?

 **Heart Check**

When I pray, worship, or serve, am I seeking God's presence or His approval? If no one saw my devotion, would I still do it with the same intensity? If no, why?

_____
_____
_____
_____
_____
_____
_____

Do I secretly believe God's love for me rises and falls with my spiritual performance? What would it take for me to stop trying to prove that I am "enough" to God?

_____
_____
_____
_____
_____
_____
_____

 **Journal Prompt**

What parts of your "spiritual life" are really about hiding your emptiness? Do your discipline mask your hunger for control, or your fear of being unworthy of love?

Chapter 9:
A Church Home Is Essential for Spiritual Growth

Nurturing Your Faith: The Role of Community in Deepening Spirituality

 Biblical Call to Community

When God calls us into a relationship with Him, He doesn't call us to walk alone—He calls us into community. Scripture is clear that gathering together with fellow believers is a vital part of spiritual growth, discipleship, and encouragement. The church is not just a place we go to—it's a spiritual family we belong to.

From the earliest days of the church, believers gathered regularly to break bread, pray, learn, and support one another in faith and in life. This rhythm of shared life built a foundation of strength, love, and purpose.

 **Scripture**

Hebrews 10:24–25 (ESV)

"And let us consider how to stir up one another to love and good works, not neglecting to meet together, as is the habit of some, but encouraging one another, and all the more as you see the Day drawing near."

Acts 2:42-47 (ESV)

"And they devoted themselves to the apostles' teaching and the fellowship, to the breaking of bread and the prayers. And awe came upon every soul, and many wonders and signs were being done through the apostles. And all who believed were together and had all things in common. And they were selling their possessions and belongings and distributing the proceeds to all, as any had need. And day by day, attending the temple together and breaking bread in their homes, they received their food with glad and generous hearts, praising God and having favor with all the people. And the Lord added to their number day by day those who were being saved."

Reflection & Exercise

Do you believe church is only a building with four walls, or could it also be when two or three are gathered in His name, wherever they are, seeking Him together?

How might your faith deepen if you stopped waiting for church to *feed* you and began seeing yourself as part of its heartbeat?

 **Heart Check**

When I think about "church", am I seeking a community that makes me comfortable or a community that makes me *more like Christ*, even when that requires surrender, correction, or discomfort?

_____
_____
_____
_____
_____
_____

How has being part of (or searching for) a church home shaped your spiritual growth, your sense of community, and your relationship with God?

_____
_____
_____
_____
_____
_____

 **Journal Prompt**

Consider moments when having, or lacking, a church home made a difference in your faith journey. What does God teach you through those experiences about connection, accountability, and love within His body?

Chapter 10:
Social Media's Influence on Your Authentic Relationship with Christ

Navigating the Digital Divide:
Cultivating Genuine Faith in a Connected World

 The Rise of Social Media Religion

We live in an age where scrolling has replaced seeking. Platforms like Instagram, TikTok, and YouTube are filled with spiritual-sounding messages, "prophetic words," and quick-fire teachings—but many are not rooted in Scripture. This is the rise of social media religion, where opinions are mistaken for truth, and spiritual formation is replaced with digital consumption.

We're being discipled by content instead of Christ. There is more social media worship than actual worship of God. Many are learning more from reels than from the Word.

 **Scripture**

2 Timothy 4:3 (ESV)

"For the time is coming when people will not endure sound teaching, but having itching ears they will accumulate for themselves teachers to suit their own passions."

 **Reflection & Exercise**

How does the content you consume affect your emotions, faith, and thought life throughout the week?

In moments of anxiety or confusion, do you instinctively reach for your phone or your Bible first? What does that reveal about where you seek comfort and clarity?

 **Heart Check**

How often do you turn to social media for spiritual guidance instead of seeking God personally in Scripture and prayer?

_____
_____
_____
_____
_____
_____
_____

Is your relationship with Christ growing stronger through online content, or is it suffering from distractions and superficial teachings?

_____
_____
_____
_____
_____
_____
_____

 # Journal Prompt

Take inventory of how much time you spend consuming spiritual content online versus spending quiet, personal time with God. Write about any patterns you notice. What specific steps can you take to prioritize authentic connection with Christ over digital noise?

 From Preachers to Performers

Social media has become a stage. Many self-appointed voices now care more about going viral than going deeper. They chase views, not victory. They perform rather than preach. It's no longer about keeping God famous—it's about being known, branded, followed, and praised.

The danger is that charisma can overshadow calling. People are building platforms on opinions rather than surrendering to God's truth.

 Scripture

Matthew 6:1 (ESV)

"Beware of practicing your righteousness before other people in order to be seen by them, for then you will have no reward from your Father who is in heaven."

Reflection & Exercise

Have you ever been more drawn to someone's presentation more than their biblical truth? What does that reveal about your spiritual appetite?

How can you discern between someone who's truly preaching Jesus and someone promoting themselves?

 **Heart Check**

Have you ever mistaken emotional impact for spiritual truth, assuming that someone's eloquence or charisma was evidence of God's anointing? How can you train your spirit to recognize the quiet authority of the Holy Spirit over the noise of human talent?

_____
_____
_____
_____
_____
_____

What hidden places in your life crave applause more than obedience, and how is that shaping your walk with Christ?

_____
_____
_____
_____
_____
_____

Misrepresenting the Called

While many chase fame, there are still pastors who are genuinely laboring for souls. But even they are not safe from distorted perception. Social media has made it easy to take thirty seconds out of a sermon and turn it into fuel for criticism and shame.

These pastors are being judged by people who never heard the full message, never sat under their teaching, and never prayed for them. In the age of content, context is ignored—and the Gospel suffers because of it.

 ## Scripture

Proverbs 18:13 (NLT)

"Spouting off before listening to the facts is both shameful and foolish."

 **Reflection & Exercise**

Am I more likely to notice faults or faithfulness in my leaders? What does that reveal about my heart?

_____
_____
_____
_____
_____
_____

What would it look like to honor, pray for, or encourage leaders who are truly doing the work of ministry?

_____
_____
_____
_____
_____
_____

 **Journal Prompt**

Write about a time when you criticized or dismissed a pastor, leader, or ministry without knowing the weight they carried or the battles they fought. How did that moment expose pride, a critical spirit, or a lack of love in your own heart?

The Gospel Was Never Meant to Shame

The Gospel brings conviction, not condemnation. But today's culture of "correction" has turned into public humiliation. Spiritual rebuke is now entertainment. People are being called out—not to bring them to Christ, but to gain clout online.

This is not the way of Jesus.

Jesus corrected in love. He never shamed the broken—He restored them. He didn't drag sinners into the light to embarrass them—He invited them into healing.

 Scripture

Galatians 6:1 (NLT)

"Dear brothers and sisters, if another believer is overcome by some sin, you who are godly should gently and humbly help that person back onto the right path. And be careful not to fall into the same temptation yourself."

 **Reflection & Exercise**

Have you participated in or supported the public shaming of others under the guise of "truth-telling"?

What does healthy, Christ-centered correction look like—and how can you model it?

 **Heart Check**

If someone were correcting *me*, how would I want them to approach it? What can that teach me about how to treat others?

 **Journal Prompt**

Think of a time when you joined in, stayed silent, or even felt satisfaction while someone was shamed or 'called out' publicly—online or in person. What did that moment reveal about your own heart and how you view other's failures?

Chapter 11:
Trusting God in the Midst of the Struggle

Finding Strength in Adversity: Embracing Faith and Hope During Life's Challenges

Trusting God completely can feel like one of the hardest things we're ever asked to do. In theory, the concept of trusting God is simple: lean not on your own understanding, surrender your plans, and let Him guide your steps. But in practice, it's anything but easy. Trusting God 100%, fully, and without reservation—requires us to release control, let go of our own fears, and embrace the unknown, even when it feels like we're walking blind.

In a world filled with uncertainty, anxiety, and fear, trusting God is often an enduring process. We hear people say, "Just trust God," but how many of us truly understand the weight of that statement? It's not a quick fix. Trusting God means facing your doubts head-on and choosing His promises over your feelings. It's surrendering your desires, your timelines, and even your understanding of how things should go. And in the midst of it all, there's often a voice—the enemy whispering doubts, trying to convince us that God isn't faithful, that He's distant, or that we can handle things better on our own. But here's the truth: the process of trusting God and letting go is often more difficult than physical labor. It takes endurance to keep choosing faith over fear, to silence the whispers of the enemy, and to remember that God is who He says He is. A lack of trust in God can delay our blessings because we remain stuck in the cycle of control, fear, and self-reliance. But when we fully trust God, we open the door to His perfect will and timing.

It's hard, but it's worth it. The process is refining, and through it, we grow closer to God, learning to lean on Him and not on our own understanding.

 Scripture

Proverbs 3:5-6 (ESV)

"Trust in the Lord with all your heart, and do not lean on your own understanding. In all your ways acknowledge Him, and He will make straight your paths."

 **Reflection & Exercise**

What are the areas in your life where you're still leaning on your own understanding instead of trusting God fully? How does this impact your peace and your walk with Him?

_____
_____
_____
_____
_____

How does Proverbs 3:5-6 challenge your current view of trust? What steps can you take to acknowledge God in all your ways and stop relying on your own understanding?

_____
_____
_____
_____
_____

 **Heart Check**

Where are you clinging to control and calling it faith?

In what ways has your lack of trust in God delayed the blessings He's been waiting to give you? What would it look like to surrender that trust today?

 # Journal Prompt

Identify the part of your life where it feels like God has gone silent, the place you've prayed over and over, yet nothing seems to change. What fears whisper louder than His promises? What wounds make you believe He won't come through for you this time?

Chapter 12:
Moving Forward with Grace, Truth, and Freedom

Embracing the Journey: Living Out Faith with Purpose, Integrity, and Liberation

 Rediscovering Your Identity in Christ

Your identity is not found in titles, performance, or perfection. It's found in the finished work of Jesus Christ. Your identity is discovered through becoming whole. As you've walked through the pages of this workbook, you've been invited to strip away religion, roles, and routine to rediscover the beauty of being a child of God— fully loved, fully seen, and fully accepted.

You are not who others say you are. You are not the mistakes you've made. You are who God says you are.

 **Scripture**

1 John 3:1 (NIV)
"See what great love the Father has lavished on us, that we should be called children of God! And that is what we are!"

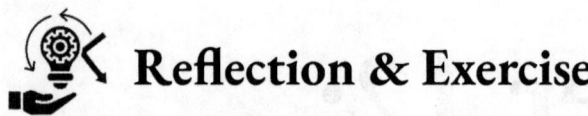# Reflection & Exercise

When you hear that you are "a new creation in Christ," what part of you resists believing that? Why?

_____
_____
_____
_____
_____
_____

What specific lies have you believed about yourself that God has been gently confronting?

_____
_____
_____
_____
_____
_____

 **Heart Check**

How have pain, trauma, or rejection rewritten how you see yourself, and what would it mean to let Christ rewrite it instead?

📓 Journal Prompt

What specific memories replay in your mind when you start to believe you're unworthy of grace and what emotion always comes with them (shame, fear, regret, anger)? How could you rewrite that story through the lens of who God says you are?

Final Prayer: Embracing Grace & Walking in Freedom

Jesus…

You see the parts of me I try to hide — the memories that still ache, the words I still replay, the moments I still regret. You see the fear I wear like armor, the guilt that whispers I'll never be enough, the shame that still tries to name me. I'm tired of pretending I'm okay. I'm tired of carrying what You already died to take from me. Step into the dark corners of my heart, Lord. Don't just visit them — overturn the tables there. Tear down every lie I've believed about who I am and what I'm worth. Let Your truth roar louder than the accusations that haunt me. Remind me that I am not my failures.

I am not my wounds. I am not what was done to me. I am who You say I am — forgiven, chosen, redeemed, and loved beyond measure. Jesus, rewrite my story with Your mercy. Take the pages soaked in regret and turn them into testimonies of grace.

Break the chains of shame, of unworthiness, of fear. Every agreement I've made with the enemy — I renounce it now in Your name. Every voice that tells me I'm too broken, too far gone — silence it with Your love.

I don't just want to believe about You — I want to know You. I want Your presence to invade every part of me until nothing remains untouched by Your healing. Make me whole, make me new, make me Yours — completely, without reservation.

Here I am, Jesus.

All of me.

Even the messy, trembling, uncertain parts.

Do what only You can do.

In Your holy and precious name,

Amen.

Appendices:
Additional Resources for Growth

Books, articles, and resources for deeper exploration on the themes of grace, identity, and church life.

 **Books**

Grace

"What's So Amazing About Grace?" — Philip Yancey

A modern classic that unpacks the scandal, beauty, and necessity of grace in a grace-starved world.

"Grace: More Than We Deserve, Greater Than We Imagine" — Max Lucado

Offers a compelling and heartfelt reminder of how grace shapes everything.

"Ragamuffin Gospel" — Brennan Manning

A bold, raw, and grace-filled reminder that God's love is for the broken and not the self-righteous.

Identity in Christ

"Victory Over the Darkness" — Neil T. Anderson

Grounded in Scripture, this book helps believers live out their identity in Christ and break spiritual strongholds.

"The Search for Significance" — Robert McGee

Deals with the lies we believe about ourselves and replaces them with the truth of who we are in Christ.

Church Life & Healthy Community

"Emotionally Healthy Church" — Peter Scazzero

Explores how church leadership and culture need emotional health to cultivate spiritual maturity.

"When Church Stops Working: A Future for Your Congregation beyond More Money, Programs, and Innovation" — Andrew Root & Blair Bertrand

A powerful critique and a hopeful vision for post-institutional Christian community life.

 Articles / Essays

"Deconstructing Faith Without Deconstructing Jesus" — Relevant Magazine.

Explores how people can rethink church and faith practices without losing their relationship with Christ.

"Legalism vs. Grace: The Church's Tug-of-War" — The Gospel Coalition.

A helpful breakdown of how legalism can sneak into church culture and how to return to a grace-based mindset.

"The Church as a Hospital for the Broken" — Desiring God.

Centers on the idea of church as a place for healing, not perfection.

 # Podcasts / Audio Teachings

"The Place We Find Ourselves" by Adam Young

Focuses on identity, healing from trauma, and spiritual wholeness from a Christian lens.

"The Next Right Thing" by Emily P. Freeman

A quiet space to reflect on life decisions and God's direction for your soul.

 # Scripture-Study Resources

Misreading Scripture with Western Eyes

Removing Cultural Blinders to Better Understanding the Bible by E. Randolph Richards and Brandon J. O'Brien

"The Bible Project" (website & YouTube)

Deep, artistic, and theology-rich breakdowns of biblical themes—including grace, identity, and community.

She Reads Truth / He Reads Truth

Beautifully designed, Scripture-first studies with strong focus on knowing God personally.

Prayer Journal Pages

Rhaegine Valero